Sich nie mehr blamieren in
ENGLISCH
Redewendungen

Werner Brandl

Compact Verlag

© 2000 Compact Verlag München

Alle Rechte vorbehalten.
Nachdruck, auch auszugsweise,
nur mit ausdrücklicher Genehmigung
des Verlages gestattet.

Chefredaktion: Ilse Hell
Redaktion: Karina Partsch
Redaktionsassistenz: Katharina Eska, Stefanie Sommer
Illustrationen: Atelier Andreas Piel
Produktionsleitung: Gunther Jaich
Umschlaggestaltung: Inga Koch
Printed in Germany
ISBN 3-8174-7162-9
7271621
Besuchen Sie uns im Internet: www.compactverlag.de

Vorwort

Jeder, der Englisch lernt, begegnet dabei früher oder später den „Idioms" – Redewendungen, die vor allem den routinierten Sprecher auszeichnen.

Viele deutsche Redewendungen können wörtlich ins Englische übersetzt und richtig angewendet werden. Es gibt jedoch auch eine ganze Reihe, bei der dies nicht so einfach möglich ist. Zum Teil rufen solche Übersetzungen dann Ratlosigkeit hervor, zum Teil bedeuten sie etwas völlig anderes. So stiften sie oft Verwirrung und führen unter Umständen zu peinlichen Missverständnissen.

Dieses Buch stellt eine Reihe häufig verwendeter und exemplarischer Redewendungen vor und erläutert jede deutsche Redewendung durch Beispielsätze und die richtige Übersetzung, wobei es oft mehrere Möglichkeiten gibt. Der situationsgemäß richtige Gebrauch wird so aufgezeigt. Durch die humorvollen Illustrationen prägen sich die meist auch sehr bildlichen Redewendungen besser ein.

Aus der großen Fülle an Redewendungen wurden für diesen Band die ausgewählt, die sich durch häufigen Gebrauch und ihre praktische Verwendbarkeit auszeichnen. Die aufgeführten Redewendungen kommen sowohl schriftlich als auch mündlich oft vor, wobei ein Schwerpunkt auf der britischen Sprache und dem eher umgangssprachlichen Stil liegt.

Wer dieses Buch aufmerksam durcharbeitet, ist gegen viele Fallen gefeit und wird sich mit seinen Sprachkenntnissen nicht mehr so leicht blamieren.

A

---
das A und O sein
---

to be the Alpha and Omega

>Beispiel:
>
>Disziplin und Talent sind das A und O einer Karriere als Pianist.
>
>*Discipline and talent are the Alpha and the Omega of a career as a piano player.*

---
sich sehr in Acht nehmen
---

to cross one's t's and dot one's i's

>Beispiel:
>
>Der Auftrag ist sehr kompliziert, aber wenn ich mich sehr in Acht nehme, sollte ich es schaffen können.
>
>*The order is very complicated but if I cross my t's and dot my i's I should be able to manage it.*

im Adamskostüm sein

1. to be in one's birthday suit
2. to be stripped to the bone
3. to be stark naked

Beispiel:

1. Stell dir vor, ging doch vor zwei Wochen ein Mann im Adamskostüm durch die Stadt.
   Just imagine, two weeks ago a man walked across town in his birthday suit.

2. Ich war etwas früher zu Hause als normalerweise, und da stand dieser Mann splitterfasernackt im Bad.
   I got home earlier than usually and there was this man standing in the bathroom stripped to the bone.

3. Wenn in Deutschland Kinder pudelnackt baden, haben die anderen Badegäste meist nichts dagegen.
   If children in Germany go swimming stark naked, the other guests at the pool usually don't take offence.

wie angegossen passen

1. to fit like a glove
2. to fit to a T

Beispiel:

1. Vor drei Jahren schenkte mir deine Mutter dieses rote Kleid. Es passt mir immer noch wie angegossen.
Three years ago your mom gave me this red dress. It still fits me like a glove.

2. Seine neue Tätigkeit im Außendienst passt zu ihm wie angegossen.
His new job as a traveling salesman fits him to a T.

in den sauren Apfel beißen

1. to swallow the (bitter) pill
2. to bite the bullet

Beispiel:

1. Manchmal hat man keine Wahl und muss einfach in den sauren Apfel beißen.
Sometimes you just don't have a choice and you simply have to swallow the pill.

2. Ich wollte mir so bald wie möglich eine Stereoanlage kaufen, also biss ich in den sauren Apfel und nahm einen Job in einem Schnellimbiss an.
I wanted to buy a stereo as soon as possible so I bit the bullet and accepted a job at a snack-bar.

ein Auge zudrücken

to turn a blind eye to something

Beispiel:

Der Türsteher sagte: „Dein Freund ist noch sehr jung, aber ich will mal ein Auge zudrücken."
The bouncer said: "Your friend is still really young but I will turn a blind eye to it."

Ähnlich:

**to turn a deaf ear to something
sich taub stellen**

Die Gäste am Nachbartisch schimpften über das unmoralische Leben unseres Pfarrers, aber ich stellte mich einfach taub.
The guests at the next table were complaining about our vicar but I just turned a deaf ear to it.

eine Augenweide sein

**1. to be a sight for sore eyes
2. to be a feast for the eyes**

Beispiel:

1. Die Inszenierung war dramaturgisch schwach, aber die Bühnenausstattung war eine Augenweide.
The production was weak in dramaturgical respect, however the stage design was a sight for sore eyes.

2. Ein tolles kaltes Büffet ist nicht nur delikat, sondern auch eine Augenweide.
A splendid cold buffet does not just taste delicious; it is a feast for the eyes, too.

---
jemanden ausnutzen
---

1. to take advantage of someone
2. to take liberties with someone

Beispiel:

1. Wenn man gutmütig ist muss man aufpassen, dass man von den anderen nicht ausgenutzt wird.
If you are good-natured you have to be careful so that you are not taken advantage of.

2. Ihr Kollege nutzte sie gnadenlos aus als ihm klar wurde, dass er sie erpressen konnte.
Her colleague took liberties with her when he realized he could blackmail her.

B

---

jemandem einen Bären aufbinden

---

1. to pull somebody's leg
2. to take somebody for a ride

Beispiel:

1. Es tut mir schon Leid, aber er lässt sich halt so leicht einen Bären aufbinden, dass man kaum widerstehen kann.
I am sorry but, as a matter of fact, pulling his leg is so easy it is hard to resist.

2. Ich dachte die ganze Zeit über, dass er es ernst meinte, dabei band er mir nur einen Bären auf.
The whole time I thought he was serious but he was just taking me for a ride.

---

das Fell verkaufen, ehe man den Bären hat

---

to count one's chickens before they are hatched

Beispiel:

Der Kaufvertrag ist noch nicht unterzeichnet. Wir sollten also ruhig bleiben und nicht das Fell verkaufen, ehe wir den Bären haben.
The contract has not been signed yet. Therefore we should stay calm and not count our chickens before they are hatched.

---

einen Besen fressen

---

to eat one's hat

Beispiel:

Wenn es wirklich wahr ist, dass in deinem Garten Außerirdische gelandet sind, fresse ich einen Besen.
If it is really true that aliens have landed in your garden, I will eat my hat.

den Besitzer wechseln

to change hands

Beispiel:

Die Kneipe hat eine schlechte Lage. Deshalb ist es wirklich kein Wunder, dass sie ständig den Besitzer wechselt.
The location of the pub is not attractive. Therefore, it is not surprising at all that it changes hands all the time.

jemandem ein Loch in den Bauch reden

to talk someone's ear/head off

Beispiel:

Das ist kein Zeichen von Sympathie – er redet jedem ein Loch in den Bauch, den er trifft.
This is no sign of affection – he talks anybody's ear off he meets.

das Blaue vom Himmel erzählen

to talk through one's hat

Beispiel:

Manche Leute können das Blaue vom Himmel erzählen und man vertraut ihnen doch.
Some people can talk through their hats and still they are trusted.

etwas durch die Blume sagen

1. to tell something in a roundabout way
2. to tell something in veiled language

Beispiel:

1. Durch die Blume hat mir mein Chef zu verstehen gegeben, dass ich damit rechnen kann, nächstes Jahr Partner zu werden.
My boss told me in a roundabout way that I can count on becoming partner next year.

2. Musstest du so plump sein? Du hättest es durch die Blume sagen sollen.
Did you need to be so blunt? You should have told it in veiled language.

böhmische Dörfer für jemanden sein

1. to be (all) Greek to somebody
2. to be like a foreign language to somebody

Beispiel:

1. Mein Allgemeinwissen ist ziemlich gut, wenn auch diese ganzen Internet-Sachen böhmische Dörfer für mich sind.
My general knowledge is fairly adequate, although all this internet stuff is Greek to me.

2. Pamela ist sehr gut in Algebra, aber Geometrie ist für sie ein böhmisches Dorf.
Pamela is very good with algebra but geometry is like a foreign language to her.

---

den Bogen heraushaben

---

to have the knack of doing something

Beispiel:

Sie hat ein Talent für das Geräteturnen. Schon nach wenigen Versuchen hatte sie den Bogen raus.
She is very talented at apparatus gymnastics. After a few attempts she had the knack of it.

---

den Braten riechen

---

to smell a rat

Beispiel:

Der Schwindel war so gut geplant, dass niemand den Braten roch
The swindle was planned so well that no one smelt a rat

um den heißen Brei herumreden

to beat about the bush

Beispiel:

Sag mir bitte ob du die Scheidung willst und rede nicht lange um den heißen Brei herum
Please, tell me if you want a divorce and stop beating about the bush

ein Buch mit sieben Siegeln

to be a closed book

>Beispiel:
>
>Wie die Börse funktioniert ist für viele Leute ein Buch mit sieben Siegeln
>*How the stock exchange works is a closed book to many people.*

in Butter sein

1. to be in apple-pie order
2. to be smooth/plain sailing

>Beispiel:
>
>1. „Brauchst du Hilfe?"
>   „Nein, ich habe die Lösung für das Problem gerade gefunden – alles in Butter."
>   *"Do you need help?"*
>   *"No, I have just found the solution for the problem – everything is in apple-pie order."*
>
>2. Nachdem ich mich auf die Prüfung mehr als sechs Monate vorbereitet hatte, war für mich alles in Butter.
>   *With six months of studying the exam was smooth/plain sailing for me.*

jemanden als üblen Charakter darstellen

to paint someone black

    Beispiel:

    Du solltest ihn nicht als so üblen Charakter darstellen, er hat auch seine guten Seiten.
    You should not paint him black, he has some good traits, too.

D

jemandem die Daumen drücken

1. to cross one's fingers
2. to keep one's fingers crossed

Beispiel:

1. Wenn wir Angela nicht die Daumen gedrückt hätten, wäre sie sicher nicht so erfolgreich gewesen.
If we had not crossed our fingers, Angela would not have been so successful.

2. Morgen habe ich meine Führerscheinprüfung – halt mir also die Daumen!
Tomorrow I am taking my driving test – keep your fingers crossed!

unter einer Decke stecken

1. to be in league
2. to be in cahoots

Beispiel:

1. Niemand wusste, dass der Bürgermeister und der Nachtclubbesitzer unter einer Decke steckten.
   Nobody knew that the mayor was in league with the owner of the night club.

2. Manche Leute sagen, der CIA und die Drogenkartelle stecken unter einer Decke.
   Some people say the CIA and the drug cartels are in cahoots.

jemandem einen Denkzettel verpassen

1. to give someone something to think about
2. to teach someone a lesson

Beispiel:

1. Herbert hat sich meiner Schwester gegenüber schäbig verhalten. Ich werde ihm einen Denkzettel verpassen.
   Herbert has treated my sister in a mean way. I am going to give him something to think about.

2. Der Parteivorsitzende beschloss, dem Mitglied, das sich so parteischädigend verhalten hatte, einen Denkzettel zu verpassen.
The party leader decided to teach a lesson to the member who had acted so detrimental to the party.

---

jemandem ein Dorn im Auge sein

---

to be a thorn in one's side

Beispiel:

Der schlechte Verdienst ihres Mannes war ihr von Beginn an ein Dorn im Auge gewesen.
From the beginning the meager earnings of her husband had been a thorn in her side.

---

wie ein Ei dem anderen gleichen

---

to be (as like) as two peas (in a pod)

    Beispiel:

    Niemand kann die Zwillinge auseinander halten, sie gleichen sich wie ein Ei dem anderen
    Nobody can tell the difference between the twins – they are as like as two peas in a pod

jemanden wie ein rohes Ei behandeln

1. to treat someone very gingerly
2. to handle someone with kid gloves

Beispiel:

1. Irene verträgt die Wahrheit, du brauchst sie nicht wie ein rohes Ei zu behandeln.
   Irene can cope with the truth so you do not need to treat her very gingerly.

2. Wenn du nicht aufhörst, deinen Sohn weiterhin mit Samthandschuhen anzufassen, wird er nie selbstständig.
   If you do not stop treating your son with kid gloves, he will never become independent.

wie auf Eiern gehen

to walk like a cat on hot bricks/tiles

Beispiel:

Wir waren nicht sicher, ob das Eis uns tragen würde, deshalb gingen wir wie auf Eiern.
We were not sure whether the ice would carry us so we walked like cats on hot bricks.

sich wie ein Elefant im Porzellanladen benehmen

to behave like a bull in a chinashop

Beispiel:

Auf der Party erzählte Peter viel dummes Zeug und verschüttete den Wein, kurz, er benahm sich wie ein Elefant im Porzellanladen.
At the party, Peter said all this rubbish and spilt the wine, in short, he behaved like a bull in a chinashop.

nicht von schlechten Eltern sein

to be not bad at all

Beispiel:

Dieser Wein ist nicht von schlechten Eltern. Hat er wirklich nicht mehr gekostet?
This wine is not bad at all. Was it really not more expensive?

ohne Ende essen können

to have hollow legs

> Luise scheint ohne Ende essen zu können, und trotzdem ist sie außergewöhnlich schlank.
> *Louise seems to have hollow legs and still she is exceptionally slender.*

Eulen nach Athen tragen

to carry coals to Newcastle (GB)

> Beispiel:
>
> Unserem Nachbarn Äpfel zu bringen ist wie Eulen nach Athen tragen. Er besitzt bereits den größten Obstgarten in der Gegend.
> *To give apples to our neighbour is to carry coals to Newcastle. He already owns the biggest orchard in the land.*

sich ins Fäustchen lachen

to laugh up one's sleeve

Beispiel:

Ich lachte mir ins Fäustchen, weil mein Vater meinen Bruder für einen Streich bestrafte, den ich ausgeheckt hatte.
I laughed up my sleeve because my father disciplined my brother for a trick that I had come up with.

in der Familie liegen

to run in the family

Beispiel:

Musikalität liegt bei ihr in der Familie. Ihr Großvater war auch ein wunderbarer Pianist.
Musical talent runs in her family. Her grandfather also was a wonderful pianist.

Farbe bekennen

1. to nail one's colours to the mast
2. to reveal one's true colours
3. to come into the open

Beispiel:

1. Als Brian sie direkt fragte, musste Thelma Farbe bekennen.
   Thelma had to nail her colours to the mast, when Brian asked her bluntly.

2. Als man Sylvias Schwindel entdeckte, musste sie Farbe bekennen und zugeben, dass sie nie Profimusikerin gewesen war.
   When Sylvia's fraud was detected she had to reveal her true colours and admit that she had never been a professional musician.

3. Wenn dich dein schlechtes Gewissen quält, solltest du einfach Farbe bekennen
   If your guilty conscience is bothering you, then just come out into the open

früh aus den Federn sein

to be up with the lark

Beispiel:

Er muss früh aus den Federn sein, um den Zug zu seiner Arbeit am anderen Ende der Stadt zu erwischen.
He must be up with the lark in order to catch the train to his job at the other side of town.

jemanden fertig machen

1. to wipe the floor with someone
2. to haul someone over the coals

Beispiel:

1. Erst lächelte der Verkaufsleiter noch, später machte er dann die Abteilungsleiter völlig fertig
At first the sales director was smilling, later on he wiped the floor with the heads of departments.

2. Den anderen Kindern erzählte Kevin, sein Vater sei Astronaut. Als sie aber die Wahrheit herausfanden, machten sie den armen Kevin fertig
Kevin told the other kids his dad was an astronaut. But when they found out the truth they hauled poor Kevin over the coals

ins Fettnäpfchen treten

1. to drop a brick
2. to put one's foot in it

Beispiel:

1. Toni trat bei der Party ins Fettnäpfchen als er enthüllte, dass die Firma bankrott war.
   At the party, Tony dropped a brick when he revealed that the company was bancrupt.

2. Ich hatte vor, den Besitzer des Nachtclubs 'Blauer Drache' zu verhaften. Ohne deine Informationen über seine Verbindungen zum Bürgermeister hätte ich mich ganz schön ins Fettnäpfchen gesetzt
   I had been planning to arrest Mr. Perkins, the owner of the night club 'Blue Dragon'. Without your information about his connections to the mayor, I would have definitely put my foot in it

wie ein Fisch im Wasser sein

to be fit as a fiddle

Beispiel:

Er war lange krank und musste sogar ins Krankenhaus. Aber jetzt ist er wieder gesund wie ein Fisch im Wasser.
He was ill for a long time and he even had to spend some time in hospital. But now he is fit as a fiddle again.

Ähnlich:

**to be like a fish out of water
sich verlassen vorkommen**

> Ohne seine Freunde kommt er sich verlassen vor.
> *Without his friends he is like a fish out of water.*

---

sich ins eigene Fleisch schneiden

**1. to cut one's own throat
2. to cut off one's nose to spite one's face**

> Beispiel:
>
> 1. Wenn Peter wieder mit dem Chef streitet, wird er sich ins eigene Fleisch schneiden.
> *If Peter has another quarrel with his boss he will cut his own throat.*
>
> 2. Ich werde mich nicht von dir scheiden lassen. So würde ich mich ins eigene Fleisch schneiden, da du das Haus und die Kinder behalten würdest.
> *I will not get a divorce from you. It would be like cutting off my nose to spite my face since you would keep the house and the children.*

---

zwei Fliegen mit einer Klappe schlagen
---

to kill two birds with one stone

Beispiel:

Du fliegst nach London und bekommst noch Geld dafür – so schlägst du zwei Fliegen mit einer Klappe.
You go to London and what's more, you even earn some money – that's killing two birds with one stone.

jemanden mit Freundlichkeiten überhäufen

to kill someone with kindness

Beispiel:

Die Familie meiner Freundin hat mich so gerne. Immer wenn wir sie besuchen überhäufen sie mich mit Freundlichkeiten.
My girl-friend's family is so accepting of me. Every time we visit them they kill me with kindness.

mit dem falschen Fuß aufstehen

to get out of bed on the wrong side

Beispiel:

Julia ist heute furchtbar zänkisch. Sie ist wohl mit dem falschen Fuß aufgestanden.
Julia is extremely quarrelsome today. She probably got out of bed on the wrong side.

jemanden am Gängelband haben

to lead somebody by the nose

Beispiel:

Thomas würde sicher gerne zum Kegeln mitkommen. Leider darf er nicht, da ihn seine Frau am Gängelband hat.
I'm sure Thomas would like to join us bowling. Unfortunately, he is not allowed to since his wife leads him by the nose.

Vorsicht:

jemanden an der Nase herumführen
to lead someone up the garden path

Die ganzen Versprechen stimmen gar nicht. Dein Zukünftiger führt dich an der Nase herum.
All those promises are not true. Your fiancé is leading you up the garden path.

Geld zum Fenster hinauswerfen

1. to pour money down the drain
2. to splash one's money about
3. to throw money away

Beispiel:

1. Dieses Auto zu kaufen wäre das Geld zum Fenster hinauszuwerfen.
   Buying this car would mean pouring money down the drain.

2. Er feiert und wirft das Geld zum Fenster raus als hätte er die Erbschaft schon.
   He makes merry and splashes the money about as if he had the inheritance already.

3. Nur weil wir im Urlaub sind heißt das noch lange nicht, dass wir das Geld zum Fenster rauswerfen müssen.
Being on a holiday does not mean that we have to throw our money away.

für etwas wie geschaffen sein

to be cut out for something

Beispiel:

John ist so glücklich mit seiner Arbeit. Für den Beruf des Radiomoderators ist er auch wie geschaffen.
John is so happy with his job. He definitely is cut out for being a host in a radio talk show.

was auch immer geschieht

come rain or shine

Beispiel:

Seine Eltern hatten gesagt: „Was auch geschieht, wir werden zu dir stehen." Und dann war es so schnell vergessen.
His parents had said: "We will stick with you, come rain or shine." And then it was forgotten so soon.

jemandem wie aus dem Gesicht geschnitten sein

to be the spitting image of someone

> Beispiel:
>
> Es ist unglaublich. Sie ist ihrer Mutter wie aus dem Gesicht geschnitten.
> *It is unbelievable. She is the spitting image of her mother.*

auf etwas Gift nehmen

to bet one's sweet life on something

> Beispiel:
>
> Er hatte gesagt: „Diese Aktien werden steigen, darauf kannst du Gift nehmen." Jetzt stehe ich mit Schulden da.
> *He had said: "These stocks will rise, you can bet your sweet life on that." Now I am in debt.*

etwas an die große Glocke hängen

to make a (great) song and dance about something

Beispiel:

Kein Wunder, dass alle Geld von ihm fordern. Was musste er seinen Lotteriegewinn auch an die große Glocke hängen.
It is hardly surprising that all people want money from him. Why did he have to make such a great song and dance about his lottery winnings.

über etwas Gras wachsen lassen
---

1. to let the dust settle on something
2. to let bygones be bygones

Beispiel:

1. Viele Politiker gehen davon aus, dass mit der Zeit Gras über ihre Verfehlungen wächst.
Many politicians expect the dust to settle on their offences in time.

2. Dass er mich damals sehr verletzt hat ist klar, aber man sollte endlich Gras über die Sache wachsen lassen.
He certainly hurt me a lot at the time but we should definitely let bygones be bygones.

---

etwas in den Griff bekommen

---

to get the hang of something

> Beispiel:
>
> Am Anfang war mein neuer Job schwierig, doch bald hatte ich alles im Griff.
> *At first my new job was difficult but soon I got the hang of it.*

Grimassen schneiden

---

to pull/make faces

Beispiel:

Seine Mutter mag ja sehr stolz auf ihn sein, aber kann der kleine Samuel denn noch etwas anderes außer Grimassen schneiden?
His mother may be very proud of him, but I really ask myself whether little Samuel has any other abilities than pulling faces.

---

jemanden grün und blau schlagen

---

to beat somebody black and blue

Beispiel:

Gordon sah wirklich schlimm aus. Die Bande hatte ihn grün und blau geschlagen.
Gordon was such a sad sight. The gang had beaten him black and blue.

ein Haar in der Suppe finden

to find a fly in the ointment

Beispiel:

Egal wie gut unser Sohn seine Hausaufgaben macht, der Lehrer findet immer ein Haar in der Suppe.
It does not matter how well our son does his homework, his teacher will always find a fly in the ointment.

die Hand/Finger im Spiel haben

1. to have a finger in the pie
2. to have a say in something

Beispiel:

1. Es ist nicht ganz klar, wer in dieser Firma letztlich die Finger im Spiel hat.
   In this company it is not clear who really has a finger in the pie.

2. John hat als Liebling des Chefs überall seine Finger im Spiel.
   John, as the boss's favourite, has a say in everything.

jemandem ins Handwerk pfuschen

to meddle in someone else's affairs

Beispiel:

Musst du mir immer ins Handwerk pfuschen? Es hätte wunderbar geklappt, wenn du nicht alles zunichte gemacht hättest.
Do you always have to meddle in my affairs? It would have worked out great if you had not messed everything up.

wissen, wie der Hase läuft

to see how the land lies

> Beispiel:
>
> Am Anfang ist die Arbeit noch schwierig, doch bald weiß man wie der Hase läuft.
> *In the beginning this work is difficult but soon you realise how the land lies.*

in jemandes Haut stecken

to be in somebody's shoes

> Beispiel:
>
> Heute hat der Chef wieder einen schlechten Tag. Da möchte ich nicht in der Haut seiner Sekretärin stecken.
> *Today the boss is bad tempered again. I would not like to be in his assistant's shoes.*

das Herz auf der Zunge haben/tragen

to wear one's heart on one's sleeve

Beispiel:

Damian ist ein herzensguter Mensch, aber manchmal gerät er in Schwierigkeiten, weil er sein Herz auf der Zunge hat.
Damian is such a good person but sometimes he gets into trouble for wearing his heart on his sleeve.

---

jemandem rutscht das Herz in die Hose

---

1. to have one's heart in one's boots
2. someone's heart goes into his boots

Beispiel:

1. Jason hatte sich vorgenommen, sich bei seiner Professorin wegen seiner Noten zu beschweren. Als er es aber versuchte, rutschte ihm das Herz in die Hose.
Jason had set his mind on complaining to his teacher about his grades, but when he attempted to, his heart was in his boots.

2. Als er seinen Gegner erblickte, rutschte ihm das Herz in die Hose.
When he caught sight of his opponent his heart went right into his boots.

etwas/jemand auf Herz und Nieren prüfen

to put something/someone through his/its paces

Beispiel:

Sie war sehr skeptisch und prüfte den Wagen erst auf Herz und Nieren, bevor sie ihn kaufte.
She was very sceptical and put the car through its paces before she bought it.

jemandem die Hölle heiß machen

1. to give someone hell
2. to make it hot for someone

Beispiel:

1. Dieser kleine Danny weigert sich in die Schule zu gehen. Ich würde ihm die Hölle heiß machen, wenn ich seine Mutter wäre.
That little Danny refuses to go to school. I would give him hell if I were his mother.

2. Wenn er das ganze Erbe verspielt, ist es kein Wunder, dass ihm seine Frau die Hölle heiß macht.
If he gambles away the whole inheritance it is not surprising that his wife makes it hot for him.

ein Herz und eine Seele sein

1. to be hand in glove with someone
2. to see eye to eye (with someone)

Beispiel:

1. Obwohl Michael und Jane schon seit acht Jahren zusammen sind, sind sie nach wie vor ein Herz und eine Seele.
Michael and Jane have been a couple for eight years and still they are hand in glove with each other.

2. Es scheint wie ein Wunder, dass sie immer noch bei allem was sie tun ein Herz und eine Seele sind, nachdem sie schon so lange verheiratet sind.
After such a long time of being married it seems like a miracle that they still see eye to eye in everything they do.

auf zwei Hochzeiten tanzen

1. to have one's cake and eat it (,too)
2. to be in more than one place at one time

1. Wenn wir das Konzert eher verlassen um noch auf die Party zu gehen, werden wir von beidem nicht viel haben. Man kann nicht auf zwei Hochzeiten tanzen.
If we leave the concert earlier in order to go to the party we won't get much of both. You can't have your cake and eat it, too.

2. „Morgen spielen meine beiden Lieblingsgruppen, und ich würde so gerne beide sehen."
„Du wirst dich entscheiden müssen, da du nicht auf zwei Hochzeiten tanzen kannst."
"Tomorrow my two favourite bands are playing and I would love to see both of them."
"You will have to make a decision as you cannot be in more than one place at one time."

aus dem gleichen Holz geschnitzt sein

to be a chip off the old block

Beispiel:

Sie sieht zwar ganz anders aus als ihre Eltern, aber vom Wesen her ist die Tochter der Masons aus dem gleichen Holz geschnitzt.
Though looking entirely different from her parents, characterwise the Masons' daughter is a chip off the old block.

auf dem Holzweg sein

1. to be on the wrong track
2. to bark up the wrong tree

Beispiel:

1. Wenn Marisa glaubt, dass ich nicht erkenne wie schlecht ihr Angebot ist, dann ist sie auf dem Holzweg.
   If Marisa thinks that I do not realise how bad her offer is, she is on the wrong tack.
2. Wenn Sie den Abteilungsleiter für den Verräter halten, sind sie auf dem Holzweg.
   If you believe the head of department to be the traitor, you are barking up the wrong tree.

---

ein Hühnchen mit jemandem zu rupfen haben

---

to have a bone to pick with someone

Beispiel:

Nach all diesen Vorfällen hat sie sicher ein Hühnchen mit ihm zu rupfen.
After all those affairs, she is sure to have a bone to pick with him.

I

eine fixe Idee haben

to have a bee in one's bonnet about something

Beispiel:

Robert geht mir wirklich auf die Nerven. Er hat die fixe Idee den nächsten Urlaub in Norwegen zu verbringen, wohingegen ich lieber in die Türkei fahren würde.
Robert is getting on my nerves. He has a bee in his bonnet about spending his next holiday in Norway, whereas I would prefer to go to Turkey.

J

---
zu allem Ja und Amen sagen
---

to say yes to everything

>Beispiel:
>
>Am liebsten von allen Kunden verhandle ich mit ihm. Er sagt zu allem Ja und Amen.
>*He is my favourite customer to negotiate with. He says yes to everything.*

Jacke wie Hose sein
---

1. to be as broad as it is long
2. to be six of one and half a dozen of the other

>Beispiel:
>
>1. Ich habe Hunger. Ob wir jetzt zum Chinesen oder zum Italiener gehen ist mir Jacke wie Hose.
>*I am hungry. It is as broad as it is long to me whether we go to the Chinese or the Italian restaurant.*

2. Ob wir den Wein um die Ecke oder im Supermarkt kaufen ist Jacke wie Hose. Er kostet überall gleich viel.
Whether we buy the wine around the corner or at the supermarket is six of one and half a dozen of the other. It is the same price anywhere.

Jägerlatein/Lügengeschichten erzählen

1. to tell tall stories
2. to tell a cock and bull story

Beispiel:

1. Natürlich klingen seine Geschichten glaubhaft, aber ein Gutteil davon ist doch nur Jägerlatein.
Of course, his stories sound credible but a big share of them are simply tall stories.

2. Jim hat sicher keine Elefantenherde in Südspanien gesehen. Er erzählt doch immer Lügengeschichten wenn er aus dem Urlaub kommt.
I am sure Jim did not see a herd of elephants in Southern Spain. He is always telling cock and bull stories when he returns from his holidays.

---

alle Jubeljahre einmal

---

once in a blue moon

Beispiel:

Die Gelegenheit Jonny Cash spielen zu sehen ergibt sich nur alle Jubeljahre einmal.
The opportunity to see Jonny Cash perform live comes around only once in a blue moon.

K

---
auf die hohe Kante legen
---

to lay away for a rainy day

    Beispiel:

    Du verdienst jetzt sehr gut. Ich glaube es wäre eine gute Idee, etwas Geld auf die hohe Kante zu legen.
    You are making good money now. I think it is a good idea to lay something away for a rainy day.

---
die Karre/den Karren aus dem Dreck ziehen
---

1. to put things straight again
2. to put things back on the rails again

    Beispiel:

1. Bei all den finanziellen Problemen dieser Firma wird es einen wirklich fähigen Manager brauchen, um die Karre wieder aus dem Dreck zu ziehen.
   With all of this company's financial problems it will take a really capable manager to put things straight again.

2. Vor der Wahl behaupten alle, die Karre aus dem Dreck ziehen zu wollen, danach geht es doch nur um den Machterhalt.
Prior to an election everyone promises to put things back on the rails again but afterwards the securing of power is the issue.

alles auf eine Karte setzen

to put all one's eggs into one basket

Beispiel:

Als Meredith merkte, dass Roger die letzte U-Bahn nehmen wollte, setzte sie alles auf eine Karte und küsste ihn einfach.
When Meredith realised that Roger wanted to take the last underground she put all her eggs into one basket and simply kissed him.

getrennte Kasse (machen)

1. to go Dutch with someone
2. to have a Dutch treat

Beispiel:

1. Das ist wirklich lieb von dir, mein Essen mitzahlen zu wollen. Aber lass uns lieber getrennte Kasse machen.
   It is really kind of you to also pay for my food. But I would prefer going Dutch with you.

2. Ich hatte mich so auf das Rendezvous gefreut, und dann besteht dieser Blödmann auf getrennte Kasse.
   I had been looking forward to the date so much but then this idiot insistes on having a Dutch treat.

etwas im Keime ersticken

1. to nip something in the bud
2. to quell something at the source

Beispiel:

1. Für gewöhnlich versuchen Diktaturen jede Art von oppositionelle Bewegungen im Keim zu ersticken.
   Usually dictatorships try to nip oppositional movements in the bud.

2. Louises Mutter hatte sie immer gezwungen, Plüschtiere zu häkeln und hatte so jede Lust auf Handarbeit im Keim erstickt.
Louise's mother used to force her to crochet cuddly toys and had thus quelled any interest in handicrafts at the source.

---

das Kind beim (rechten) Namen nennen

---

to call a spade a spade

Beispiel:

Sie nennen es Wahlkampfspenden, aber wenn wir das Kind beim rechten Namen nennen, dann ist es einfach Bestechung.
They call it campaign contributions but, if we call a spade a spade, it is simply bribery.

---

die Kirche im/beim Dorf lassen

---

1. to draw the line somewhere
2. not to get carried away
3. to keep within bounds

Beispiel:

1. Natürlich müssen wir den Gästen etwas Eindrucksvolles servieren. Dennoch sollten wir die Kirche im Dorf lassen und auf die Kaviarhäppchen verzichten.
Certainly we must serve something impressive to our guests. Still we should draw the line somewhere and do without the caviar appetizers.

2. Bei der Auswahl des Hochzeitsautos sollten wir die Kirche im Dorf lassen. Ein Rolls Royce ist nicht notwendig, ein Volvo reicht völlig.
With the selection of the wedding car we should not get carried away. A Rolls Royce is not necessary – a Volvo will do the job perfectly.

3. Ich bitte dich die Kirche im Dorf zu lassen. Wegen deines Auftritts beim Schulkonzert brauchst du nicht noch einen neuen Anzug.
Please, keep within bounds. You really do not need a new suit for the school concert.

jemandem einen Knüppel zwischen die Beine werfen

1. to put a spoke in somebody's wheel
2. to throw a spanner in(to) the works

Beispiel:

1. Egal was Peter versucht, seine Gegner werfen ihm immer Knüppel zwischen die Beine.
Regardless of what it is that Peter attempts, his opponents always put a spoke in his wheel.

2. Es ist schwierig in diesem Geschäft voranzukommen, wo unsere Konkurrenten uns wirklich ständig Knüppel zwischen die Beine werfen.
It is difficult to get ahead in this business because our competitors are constantly throwing spanners into our works.

---

den Kürzeren ziehen

---

1. to be left out in the cold
2. to get the short end of the stick

Beispiel:

1. Manchmal muss man sich schon beschweren, sonst zieht man den Kürzeren.
Sometimes you just have to complain, otherwise you will be left out in the cold.

2. Immer wenn er mit seinem großen Bruder stritt, zog er den Kürzeren.
Each time he quarelled with his elder brother he got the short end of the stick.

sich vor Lachen biegen

to burst laughing

    Beispiel:

    Die Clownnummer im Zirkus war so lustig, dass wir uns vor Lachen bogen.
    The clown part of the circus show was so funny that we burst laughing.

mit seinem Latein am Ende sein

1. to be at one's wit's end
2. to be at the end of the tether

Beispiel:

1. Die Prüfung war schwerer als ich erwartet hatte. Ich war bald mit meinem Latein am Ende.
   The exam turned out to be harder than I had expected. Soon I was at my wit's end.

2. Ich kann verstehen, dass sie mit ihrem Latein am Ende ist, wo sie zwei Jobs hat und immer noch nicht genug Geld zum Leben.
   I can understand that she is at the end of the tether with two jobs and still not enough money to make a living.

etwas mit links machen

1. to be able to do something blindfold(ed)
2. to be able to do something standing on one's head
3. to be able to do something with one arm tied behind one's back

Beispiel:

1. Wolfgang spielt schon so lange Klavier, dass er diese Mozart-Sonate mit links spielen kann.
   Wolfgang has played the piano for so long that he is able to play this Mozart sonata blindfold(ed).

2. Diese Mathematikklasse ist so einfach, dass ich meine Hausaufgaben mit links machen kann.
This math class is so easy I can do my homework standing on my head.

3. Ich weiß so viel über VWs, dass ich deinen Motor mit links überholen könnte.
I know so much about Volkswagens that I could overhaul your engine with one arm tied behind my back.

sein eigenes Loblied singen

to blow one's own trumpet

Beispiel:

Nach einer Weile waren die Freunde von Robert ziemlich genervt, weil er immer sein eigenes Loblied sang was seinen Job betraf.
After a while, Robert's friends got rather annoyed because he always blew his own trumpet concerning his job.

die Luft ist rein

the coast is clear

Beispiel:

Als er den unsicheren Blick von Dick bemerkte sagte John lachend: „Die Luft ist rein, Mary ist vor einer Stunde gegangen".
When he noticed Dick's nervous glance, John laughed and said, "the coast is clear, Mary left an hour ago."

jemandem gründlich die Meinung sagen

to give somebody a piece of one's mind

Beispiel:

Obwohl sie sich fest vorgenommen hatte, ihm diesmal gründlich die Meinung zu sagen, vergaß sie ihren Ärger sofort als er an der Tür über das ganze Gesicht strahlte.
Although she was set on giving him a piece of her mind she immediately forgot about her anger when he was all smiles at the door.

seinen Meister finden

to meet one's match

Beispiel:

Im Gymnasium war ich der beste Schachspieler, doch im College fand ich meinen Meister.
At grammar school I was the best chess player but at college I met my match.

das Menschenmögliche tun

to do one's (level) best

>Beispiel:
>
>Ihr sollten keine Vorwürfe gemacht werden, da sie nicht verantwortlich für die schrecklichen Folgen war. Sie hatte das Menschenmögliche getan.
>*She should not be accused as she was not responsible for the terrible consequences. She had done her (level) best.*

jemandem das Messer an die Kehle setzen

to hold a pistol to somebody's head

Beispiel:

Simon hätte seine Arbeit nie erledigt, wenn der Chef ihm nicht das Messer an die Kehle gesetzt hätte.
Simon would have never finished his work if the boss had not put a pistol to his head.

gute Miene zum bösen Spiel machen

1. to grin and bear it
2. to put on a brave face/front

Beispiel:

1. Martin lud Peggy in eine schöne Bar ein. Als der Kellner viel mehr verlangte als er erwartet hatte, machte er gute Miene zum bösen Spiel und ließ noch ein Trinkgeld da.
Martin invited Peggy to a nice bar. When the waiter charged far more than he had expected he grinned and bore it – and even left a tip.

2. Auch in einer unerträglichen Situation ist es manchmal am besten, gute Miene zum bösen Spiel zu machen.
Even with an unbearable situation it is sometimes best to put on a brave face/front.

einen Mordshunger haben

to be so hungry one could eat a whole horse

Beispiel:

Joe hatte den ganzen Tag im Garten gearbeitet und danach hatte er einen Mordshunger.
Joe had worked in the garden all day long and afterwards he was so hungry he could eat a whole horse.

---

aus einer Mücke einen Elefanten machen

---

to make a mountain out of a molehill

Beispiel:

Ich möchte nicht aus einer Mücke einen Elefanten machen, aber das Fenster, das dein Sohn gestern eingeworfen hat, musst du ersetzen.
I do not want to make a mountain out of a molehill but you must replace the window your son smashed yesterday.

ein gutes Mundwerk haben

to have the gift of the gab

Beispiel:

Steve ist der erfolgreichste Verkäufer im ganzen Laden, weil er ein gutes Mundwerk hat. Er verkauft mehr Fotoapparate als alle anderen.
Steve is the most successful clerk in the whole shop because he has the gift of the gab. He sells more cameras than any other clerk.

auf/unter den Nägeln brennen

1. to be itching/burning to get on with something
2. to be preying on one's mind

Beispiel:

1. Nach sechs Monaten Abwesenheit brannte es mir unter den Nägeln, meine Familie und meine Freunde zu Hause wieder zu sehen.
After being away for six months I was itching to see my family and friends back home.

2. Elisa war froh, dass das Thema, das ihr schon lange unter den Nägeln brannte, endlich angesprochen wurde.
Elisa was happy to see that the topic that had been preying on her mind was finally being addressed.

sich in die Nesseln setzen

1. to get into hot water
2. to put oneself in a spot
3. to put one's foot in it

Beispiel:

1. Wenn du jetzt eine Gehaltserhöhung forderst, setzt du dich in die Nesseln.
You will get into hot water if you ask for a pay rise right now.

2. Mit einer Bemerkung über Umweltschutz wirst du dich bei der Werksleitung der Ölraffinerie in die Nesseln setzen.
If you make a remark on protecting the environment, you will put yourself in a spot with the oil refinery's management.

3. Als er Mary sagte, sie habe zugenommen, setzte er sich ganz schön in die Nesseln.
When he told Mary that she had gained weight he really put his foot in it.

auf Nummer sicher gehen

to play it safe

>Beispiel:
>
>Edward gewann 200 Dollar am Black Jack Tisch. Danach wollte er unbedingt Roulette ausprobieren, aber er beschloss auf Nummer sicher zu gehen und seinen Gewinn zu behalten.
>*Edward made $ 200 at the black jack table. After that he had an urge to give roulette a try, but he decided to play it safe and keep his winnings.*

Oberwasser haben

1. to be top dog
2. to rule the roost
3. to have the upper hand
4. to be king of the hill/mountain/castle

Beispiel:

1. Nach Erfolgen in Gesprächen mit den Politikern aus Transglobalia, hat der Vizepräsident Oberwasser.
After having been successful in talks with the politicians from Transglobalia, the vice-president is top dog.

2. In meiner Schulklasse hat nicht der stärkste Schüler Oberwasser, sondern der, der die teuersten Videospiele hat.
In my class it is not the strongest pupil who rules the roost but the one with the most expensive video games.

3. In einer Gruppe hat nicht unbedingt die intelligenteste Person Oberwasser, es kann auch einfach die lauteste sein.
In a group it is not always the smartest person who has the upper hand, it may just be the loudest.

4. Als Fred in Französisch eine Eins bekam, hatte er wieder Oberwasser.
When Fred got an A in French, he was king of the hill.

---

sich aufs Ohr legen

---

1. to get some shuteye
2. to catch some z's **(US)**

Beispiel:

1. Die Fahrt war anstrengend. Ich werde mich jetzt aufs Ohr legen und mich etwas erholen.
The trip was exhausting. Now I will get some shuteye and recover a little.

2. Es war ein langer Tag. Statt heute Abend auszugehen, lege ich mich lieber aufs Ohr.
It's been a long day. Instead of going out tonight I prefer to catch some z's.

---

die Ohren spitzen

---

to prick up one's ears

Beispiel:

Was ich jetzt sage ist sehr wichtig. Also spitzt alle die Ohren!
What I am going to tell you now is essential. So prick up your ears!

die Ohren steif halten

to keep a stiff upper lip

Beispiel:

Als sie ihr Zuhause verließ und auf die Universität ging, sagte ihr Vater zu ihr, sie solle die Ohren steif halten.
When she left home and went to university, her dad told her to keep a stiff upper lip.

viel um die Ohren haben

1. to be up to the eyes in work
2. to have a lot on one's plate

Beispiel:

1. Der Abteilungsleiter hat im Moment viel um die Ohren und kann sich deshalb nicht um die Reklamation kümmern.
   At the moment the head of the department is up to the eyes in work. That is why he cannot take care of the complaint personally.

2. Sie hatte so viel um die Ohren und dachte sich: „Lange halte ich das nicht mehr aus, dann werde ich verrückt."
   She had a lot on her plate and thought to herself "I won't stand this much longer, I will go mad."

---
unter dem Pantoffel stehen
---

1. to be a henpecked husband
2. to be under petticoat rule

    Beispiel:

    1. Bei den Petersons hat die Frau die Hosen an, ihr Mann steht unter dem Pantoffel.
At the Petersons' Judith is wearing the trousers – Paul is a henpecked husband.

    2. Manchmal tut mir der nette Mann von Frau Bell leid, weil er so unter dem Pantoffel steht.
Sometimes I feel sorry for Mrs. Bell's nice husband because he is under petticoat rule.

---
für einen Pappenstiel kaufen
---

1. to buy for a (mere) song
2. to buy for next to nothing

Beispiel:

1. Dieser Ring sieht sündhaft teuer aus, doch ich habe ihn bei einem Pfandleiher für einen Pappenstiel gekauft.
This ring looks shockingly expensive but, in fact, I bought it for a song at a pawnshop.

2. Wenn du immer handelst und alles für einen Pappenstiel kaufen willst, darfst du dich nicht über verärgerte Händler wundern.
If you always bargain and want to buy stuff for next to nothing, you must not be astonished about annoyed dealers.

---

zusammenhalten wie Pech und Schwefel

to be as thick as thieves

Beispiel:

Marina und ihre Freundin Monica zu trennen ist kaum möglich, sie halten zusammen wie Pech und Schwefel.
To separate Marina and her friend Monica is hardly possible – they are as thick as thieves.

---

nach jemandes Pfeife tanzen

1. to dance to somebody's tune
2. to play someone's game

Beispiel:

1. Da wir alle von ihm abhängig sind, ist es kein Wunder, dass jeder nach seiner Pfeife tanzt.
   As all of us are dependent on him it is not surprising that everyone dances to his tune.

2. Der Leiter unseres Pfadfinderlagers ist wirklich doof. Er hat weniger Ahnung als wir, aber trotzdem müssen wir nach seiner Pfeife tanzen.
   The leader of our boy scout camp is really stupid. He is less knowledgeable than we are but still we have to play his game.

---

das Pferd beim Schwanz aufzäumen

---

to put the cart before the horse

Beispiel:

Eine Reiseroute zu planen ohne zu wissen, ob überhaupt genug Geld für einen Urlaub da sein wird, das ist wirklich das Pferd beim Schwanz aufzäumen.
To plan an itinerary for a holiday without knowing whether there will be enough money is to put the cart before the horse.

---

keinen Pfifferling wert sein

---

not to be worth a straw/penny/cent

Beispiel:

Der Ring sieht zwar gut aus, doch er ist keinen Pfifferling wert. Als Geschenk hätte ich mir etwas weniger Billiges erwartet.
The ring may look attractive, however, it is not worth a straw. As a present I would have expected something more expensive.

---

seine Pflicht und Schuldigkeit tun

---

1. to do one's bit
2. to chip in
3. to pull one's weight

Beispiel:

1. Da die Küche unvorstellbar aussieht, sollte jeder von uns seine Pflicht und Schuldigkeit tun und beim Aufräumen helfen.
   As the kitchen is in a terrible mess, everyone of us should do his bit to help clean up.

2. Wenn jeder seine Pflicht und Schuldigkeit tut, sollten wir das Haus recht schnell reparieren können.
If everybody chips in, we should be able to repair the house relatively quickly.

3. Eine Fußballmannschaft wird nicht sehr erfolgreich sein, wenn nicht jeder seine Pflicht und Schuldigkeit tut.
A soccer team will not be very successful unless everybody on the team pulls their own weight.

am falschen Platz sein

to be a square peg in a round hole

Beispiel:

Richard ist so lebhaft und kommunikativ, dass er im Finanzamt völlig am falschen Platz ist.
Richard is so lively and talkative that in the revenue office he is a square peg in a round hole.

von Pontius zu Pilatus laufen

to go from pillar to post

Beispiel:

Für besondere Platten der Beatles muss man von Pontius zu Pilatus laufen und findet sie doch nicht immer.
For special records of the Beatles you have to go from pillar to post and still there is sometimes no way of finding them.

mit jemandem kurzen Prozess machen

to give somebody short shrift

Beispiel:

Mit Leuten, die nicht bereit sind, die Forderungen des Syndikates zu erfüllen, wird häufig kurzer Prozess gemacht.
People who are not ready to fulfill the syndicate's demands are often given short shrift.

etwas aus erster Quelle haben

1. to hear it straight from the horse's mouth
2. to have something from the source

Beispiel:

1. Ich weiß, dass Georg nächsten Monat wegzieht. Ich habe es aus erster Quelle.
I know that George is moving away next month. I heard it straight from the horse's mouth.

2. Ich habe aus erster Quelle, dass du bald befördert wirst. Der Chef erzählte es mir letzte Woche.
I have it straight from the source that you will get promoted soon. The boss told me so last week.

R

stehlen wie ein Rabe

to thieve like a magpie

Beispiel:

Wenn mir nur jemand erklären könnte, warum dieser Junge aus reichem Hause stiehlt wie ein Rabe, wo er sich doch alles kaufen könnte, was er will.
If only somebody could tell me why this boy of such prosperous offspring steals like a magpie even though he is capable of buying anything he wants.

das fünfte Rad am Wagen sein

1. to be the third wheel (at the cart)
2. to be the odd man out
3. to feel like a gooseberry

Beispiel:

1. Ich freute mich darauf mit meinem Freund Jim tanzen zu gehen, aber als er mit seiner neuen Freundin kam, war ich die ganze Nacht das fünfte Rad am Wagen.
I was excited about going out dancing with my friend Jim but when he came with his new girlfriend, I felt like a third wheel all night long.

2. Sie hatten eine lebhafte Unterhaltung über Hip-Hop Musik. Da mich diese Art Musik nie interessiert hat, fühlte ich mich wie das fünfte Rad am Wagen.
They were having a lively conversation about hip-hop music. I have never been interested in that type of music so I felt like the odd man out.

3. Den ganzen Abend fühlte sie sich allein. Sie fühlte sich wie das fünfte Rad am Wagen, denn sie war nur aus Höflichkeit eingeladen worden.
She did not have any fun at the party. She felt like a gooseberry because she had only been invited for courtesy reasons.

so recht und schlecht

after a fashion

> Beispiel:
>
> Als ich mir den Film, den du mir empfohlen hast, im französischen Original ansah, verstand ich nur so recht und schlecht um was es ging.
> *When I watched the film you recommended to me in its original French version, I was able to understand what was going on only after a fashion.*

vom Regen in die Traufe kommen

to jump/fall/leap out of the frying-pan into the fire

Beispiel:

Sie hatte sich von Mark scheiden lassen, weil er sie zu sehr einengte. Doch mit ihrem neuen Mann scheint sie nur vom Regen in die Traufe gekommen zu sein.
She had got divorced from Mark because he constricted her. However, regarding her new husband she seems to have jumped out of the frying-pan into the fire.

jemanden/etwas nicht riechen können

not to be able to stand something/somebody

Beispiel:

Obwohl er mich immer höflich behandelt hat, kann ich ihn einfach nicht riechen.
Although he has always treated me politely, I simply cannot stand him.

schimpfen wie ein Rohrspatz

to swear like a fishwife/sailor

Beispiel:

Nur weil ich ein bisschen später gekommen bin, brauchst du nicht zu schimpfen wie ein Rohrspatz.
Just because I was a little late there is no reason for swearing like a fishwife.

S

in Saus und Braus leben

1. to live on/off the fat of the land
2. to live it up

Beispiel:

1. Ihr Lotteriegewinn erlaubte ihr, ihre Arbeit aufzugeben und in Saus und Braus zu leben.
Winning the jackpot enabled her to quit her job and live on the fat off the land.

2. Ich bin nicht sicher ob es eine gute Idee ist, die nächsten zehn Jahre hart zu arbeiten und danach in Saus und Braus zu leben. Du wirst nicht mehr der gleiche sein, der du jetzt bist.
I don't think it's a good idea to work hard for the next ten years and live it up afterwards. You will not be the same person you are now.

sein Schäfchen ins Trockene bringen

1. to feather one's nest
2. to make one's pile
3. to line one's own pocket

Beispiel:

1. Viele Autohändler sind mehr oder weniger kompetent – immer aber wollen sie ihr Schäfchen ins Trockene bringen.
Many car dealers are more or less competent. What they always want to do, however, is feather their own nests.

2. Moral und Nächstenliebe sind schon wichtig, doch man muss auch sein Schäfchen ins Trockene bringen.
Morals and charity are quite important. Still you have to make your pile.

3. Kurz bevor die ganze Affäre aufflog brachte er noch sein Schäfchen ins Trockene.
Shortly before the whole scandal became public, he lined his own pocket.

über seinen Schatten springen

to swallow one's pride

Beispiel:

Es dauerte eine Weile bis Rodney über seinen Schatten sprang und seiner Frau sagte, dass er wieder gespielt und am Pokertisch ihr Auto verloren hatte.
It took Rodney some time to swallow his pride and confess to his wife that he had been gambling again and that he had lost their car at the poker table.

ein Schaumschläger sein

to be a wind-bag

Beispiel:

Peter behauptet immer, er könne alles. Dabei ist er nur ein Schaumschläger. Sobald du ihn um Hilfe bittest, hat er keine Ahnung.
Peter is always bragging that he can do anything. However, he is only a wind-bag. As soon as you ask him for help, he does not have a clue.

---

aus etwas nicht schlau/klug werden

to be unable to make head or tail of something

Beispiel:

Die meisten Leute werden aus den Steuergesetzen nicht schlau. Sie sind viel zu kompliziert.
Most people cannot make head or tail of the tax laws. They are far too complicated.

---

die Schliche kennen

to know the ropes

Beispiel:

Trotz seiner 18 Jahre kennt er alle Schliche des Versicherungsgeschäfts.
In spite of his young age, he knows the ropes of the insurance business.

jemanden zur Schnecke machen

1. to have a real go at someone
2. to tear somebody to pieces

Beispiel:

1. Als Tom herausfand, dass Marc sein Geld genommen hatte, machte er ihn zur Schnecke.
   When Tom found out that Marc had taken his money, he had a real go at him.

2. Als die anderen Kinder erfuhren, dass ihr Freund Kenny sie verpetzt hatte, machten sie ihn völlig zur Schnecke.
   When the other kids heard that their friend Kenny had told on them, they tore him to pieces.

sich freuen wie ein Schneekönig

to be as pleased as Punch

Beispiel:

Als Jonny erfuhr, dass er in dem Wettbewerb ein Auto gewonnen hatte, freute er sich wie ein Schneekönig.
When Jonny learnt that he had won a car in the contest, he was pleased as Punch.

seinen Senf dazugeben

1. to put/stick one's oar in
2. to put in one's (own) two bits

Beispiel:

1. Kann er nicht mal seinen Mund halten? Muss er denn zu allem seinen Senf dazugeben?
Can't he ever keep his mouth shut? Does he have to put his oar in everything?

2. Zu guter Letzt müssen wir es noch dem Aufsichtsrat vorlegen. Der will sicher auch seinen Senf dazugeben.
Finally we have to present it to the board of directors. I am sure they also want to put in their two bits.

den Schein wahren

to keep up appearances

Beispiel:

Obwohl Helen und Erik gerade gestritten hatten, wahrten sie bei dem wichtigen Geschäftsessen von Helen den Schein.
Although Helen and Erik had quarelled shortly before they kept up appearances at Helens's important business dinner.

mit jemandem Schindluder treiben

to play fast and loose with someone

>Beispiel:
>
>Wenn man sehr gutmütig ist, kann es auch passieren, dass andere Schindluder mit einem treiben.
>*If you are very good-natured, it is possible that other people may play fast and loose with you.*

schlafen wie ein Murmeltier

to sleep like a log/top

>Beispiel:
>
>Als ich gestern Abend endlich ins Bett kam war ich so müde, dass ich wie ein Murmeltier schlief.
>*I was so tired last night that, when I finally got to bed, I slept like a log.*

sich wie warme Semmeln/Brötchen verkaufen

to sell like hot cakes

Beispiel:

Der Erfolg unserer neuen Puppe hat unsere größten Erwartungen übertroffen. Sie verkauft sich wie warme Semmeln.
The success of our new doll has surpassed our wildest expectations. It sells like hot cakes.

---

einen Spaß verstehen

---

to be able to take a joke

Beispiel:

Ralph ist echt ein toller Kerl, aber er versteht keinen Spaß.
Ralph is a pretty great guy but he can't take a joke.

---

den Spieß umdrehen

---

to turn the tables

Beispiel:

Vor ein paar Jahren, als Herr Berg mein Chef war, behandelte er mich sehr schlecht. Seither bin ich so oft befördert worden dass ich nun den Spieß umdrehen kann.
A few years ago, when Mr. Berg was my boss, he treated me very badly. Since then I have been promoted so much that I can turn the tables now.

springlebendig sein

to be full of beans

>Beispiel:
>
>Keiner hatte erwartet, dass der kleine Benjamin schon so kurze Zeit nach der Entlassung aus dem Krankenhaus wieder springlebendig sein würde.
>*Nobody had expected little Benjamin to be full of beans so soon after getting out of the hospital.*

sich aus dem Staub machen

1. to take to one's heels
2. to show a clean pair of heels

Beispiel:

1. Bevor die Verkäuferin noch den Ladendetektiv alarmieren konnte, hatte sich der Ladendieb schon mit den gestohlenen CDs aus dem Staub gemacht.
Before the saleslady could even alert the store detective, the shoplifter had already taken to his heels with the stolen CDs.

2. Die Bankräuber machten sich aus dem Staub bevor die Polizei ankam.
The bank robbers showed a clean pair of heels before the police arrived.

---

jemandem einen Strich durch die Rechnung machen

---

to upset the apple-cart

Beispiel:

Der Entführer hatte alles perfekt geplant. Doch die Polizei machte ihm einen Strich durch die Rechnung.
The hijacker had planned everything perfectly. Nevertheless, the police upset the apple-cart.

---

zwischen den Stühlen sitzen

---

to sit on the fence

Beispiel:

Es ist weit verbreitet, dass Politiker zwischen den Stühlen sitzen, wenn es um streitbare Themen geht.
Politicians often sit on the fence when it comes to controversial issues.

---

ein Sturm im Wasserglas

---

1. a tempest in a tea-pot
2. a storm in a tea-cup

Beispiel:

1. Die ganze Aufregung um den angeblichen Skandal war nur ein Sturm im Wasserglas.
   All the fuss about the alleged scandal was only a tempest in a tea-pot.

2. Die Behauptung, dass es im öffentlichen Dienst Korruption gäbe, entpuppte sich als Sturm im Wasserglas.
The claim that there was corruption in the civil service turned out to be a storm in the tea-cup.

T

in den Tag hineinleben

1. to live in the here and now
2. to live for the present

Beispiel:

1. Manchmal ist es schwer zu entscheiden, ob man einfach in den Tag hinein leben soll oder doch die Zukunft planen.
Sometimes it is hard to decide whether to simply live in the here and now or to make plans for the future.

2. Wenn jemand so in den Tag hineinlebt wie John, sind zukünftige Umweltentwicklungen nicht von Belang.
If someone lives for the present as John does, future environmental developments are not of importance.

wie Tag und Nacht sein

to be (as) like (as) chalk and cheese

Beispiel:

Obwohl sie sich so ähnlich sehen sind Nadja und ihre Schwester im Wesen verschieden wie Tag und Nacht.
Although they look so much alike, Nadja and her sister are like chalk and cheese characterwise.

---

jemanden auf frischer Tat ertappen

to catch someone red-handed

Beispiel:

Wenn jemand im Kaufhaus beim Einstecken von Waren beobachtet wird, dann ist er auf frischer Tat ertappt.
If someone is seen stuffing goods into his pockets in a department store, he is caught red-handed.

---

in Teufels Küche kommen

to be in hot water

Beispiel:

Der Sohn von Frau Pott ist in Teufels Küche, weil er zum dritten Mal in einem Kaufhaus beim Stehlen von Armbanduhren erwischt wurde.
Mrs. Pott's son is in hot water because he was caught stealing wristwatches in a department store for the third time.

jemanden zum Teufel jagen

1. to send someone packing
2. to give someone the (order of the) boot

Beispiel:

1. Als Elenas Mann zum fünften Mal fremdgegangen war, jagte sie ihn zum Teufel.
   When Elena's husband had cheated on her for the fifth time she sent him packing.

2. Er hat sich sehr ungezogen und respektlos verhalten. Das muss ich in meinem Haus nicht dulden, deshalb schickte ich ihn in die Wüste.
   He behaved in a very rude and disrespectful manner. I do not have to tolerate that in my house, so I gave him the boot.

reinen Tisch machen

1. to make a clean sweep of something
2. to get something off one's chest

Beispiel:

1. Es wäre besser gewesen gleich am Anfang reinen Tisch zu machen. Mit jedem Tag wird alles schlimmer, und irgendwann kommt alles heraus.
It would have been better to make a clean sweep right at the beginning. Every day things get worse and worse and one day everything will come out.

2. Mein schlechtes Gewissen plagt mich seit Monaten. Ich muss reinen Tisch machen und meiner Freundin sagen, dass ich eine Affäre hatte.
My guilty conscience has been troubling me for months. I have to get this off my chest and tell my girl-friend that I had had an affair.

ein Tropfen auf den heißen Stein sein

to be a drop in the ocean

Beispiel:

Gleichgültig wie viel Geld sie für die Überlebenden des Hurrikans sammeln, es wird nur ein Tropfen auf den heißen Stein sein.
Regardless of how much money they collect for the survivors of the hurricane – it will just be a drop in the ocean.

der Tropfen, der das Fass zum Überlaufen bringt

the last straw (that broke the camel's back)

Beispiel:

Der Chef schrie: „Frau Lindberg, sie sind heute zum achten Mal zu spät zur Arbeit gekommen. Das ist der Tropfen, der das Fass zum Überlaufen gebracht hat. Sie sind gefeuert!"
The boss yelled: "Mrs. Lindberg, today is the eigth time you have come to work late. This is the last straw. You are fired!"

mit der Tür ins Haus fallen

1. to blurt it out
2. to give the show away at once

Beispiel:

1. Natürlich wollen wir das Haus letztlich kaufen, aber musstest du gleich mit der Tür ins Haus fallen?
   Of course, in the end we want to buy the house but did you have to blurt it out immediately?

2. Ich schätze seine Offenheit, wenn es auch manchmal gut wäre, nicht gleich mit der Tür ins Haus zu fallen.
   I appreciate his frankness, although at times it is not such a good idea to give the show away at once.

jemanden vor die Tür setzen

1. to throw someone into the street
2. to turn/throw somebody out

Beispiel:

1. Nachdem er zwei Monate mit der Miete im Rückstand war, setzte ihn sein Vermieter auf die Straße.
   After being two months late on the rent his landlord threw him into the street.

2. Robert trank zu viel und wurde laut und ungemütlich. Als er damit anfing, mit Bierflaschen zu werfen, setzte ihn der Kneipenwirt vor die Tür.
   Robert drank too much, and became loud and rowdy. When he started throwing beer bottles the pub-owner turned/threw him out.

etwas ohne Umschweife sagen

not to mince matters/words

Beispiel:

Ohne Umschweife sagte sie ihren neuen Nachbarn, dass sie gerne Partys feiere und es manchmal laut werden würde.
She did not want to mince words so she told her new neighbours right away that she liked to have parties and that it would get loud at times.

in anderen Umständen sein

1. to be in the family way
2. to be expecting

Beispiel:

1. Christina muss sich neue Kleider anschaffen, denn sie ist in anderen Umständen.
   Christina must purchase new clothes for she is in the family way.

2. Es ist wirklich kein Wunder, dass Andrea so eigenartige Essenskombinationen mag, sie ist ja auch in anderen Umständen.
It is no surprise at all that Andrea likes very strange combinations of food because she is expecting.

aussehen, als könnte man kein Wässerchen trüben

to look as though butter would not melt in one's mouth

Beispiel:

Die kleine Susi sah aus als könne sie kein Wässerchen trüben, doch tatsächlich war sie die Anführerin der Gang in ihrem Viertel.
Little Susi looked as though butter would not melt in her mouth but actually she was the leader of the gang in her neighbourhood.

V

verraten und verkauft sein

1. to be done for
2. to have had it

   Beispiel:

   1. Als sein Schwindel aufflog war er verraten und verkauft. Alle seine Kunden verklagten ihn.
   When his fraud was detected he was done for. All of his customers took him to court.

   2. Unsere Gläubiger wollen das Geld nächste Woche und wenn wir nicht im Lotto den Jackpot gewinnen, dann sind wir verraten und verkauft.
   Our creditors want the money next week and if we do not hit the jackpot in the lottery we have had it.

in der Versenkung verschwinden

1. to disappear into thin air
2. to vanish like magic

Beispiel:

1. Vanessa freute sich Lisa wieder zu treffen, die seit der Schule in der Versenkung verschwunden zu sein schien.
Vanessa was happy to meet Lisa again, who had disappeared into thin air since her school days.

2. Maria traf ihren Traummann in der Disco. Sie tauschten tiefe Blicke aus und tanzten zusammen. Als sie aber mit zwei Tequila Sunrise von der Bar zurückkam, war er in der Versenkung verschwunden.
Maria met the man of her dreams in a disco. They exchanged deep glances and danced together. But when she returned from the bar with two tequila sunrises he had vanished like magic.

den Vogel abschießen

1. to carry off the prize
2. to take the cake/biscuit

Beispiel:

1. Mit seiner Bemerkung über die Geliebte des Vize-Präsidenten hat der Gesandte wirklich den Vogel abgeschossen.
With his remark on the vice-president's lover the envoy really carried off the prize.

2. Wenn du bei der Party den Vogel abschießen möchtest, dann solltest du Dolly Parton imitieren.
If you want to take the cake at the party you should impersonate Dolly Parton.

vornehm tun

to give oneself/put on airs

Beispiel:

Nur weil er im Kaninchenzüchterverein die Kreismedaille gewonnen hat, glaubt er immer ganz vornehm tun zu können.
Just because he won the county medal of the rabbit breeders' club he thinks he can give himself airs.

sich jemanden warm halten

1. to stay in somebody's good books
2. to keep in with somebody

Beispiel:

1. Du solltest sie dir auf jeden Fall warm halten, vielleicht brauchst du einmal ihre Hilfe.
   In any case you should stay in her good books, maybe you will need her help some time in the future.

2. Um ein soziales Netzwerk aufrechtzuerhalten, sollte man sich auch Bekannte, die man nicht sehr häufig trifft, warm halten.
   To maintain a social network one shoud try to also keep in with acquaintances one does not meet very often.

mit allen Wassern gewaschen sein

1. to be sharp as a needle
2. to be a shrewd/cool customer
3. to know all the tricks

Beispiel:

1. Obwohl Gabriel noch ein kleiner Junge ist, ist er doch mit allen Wassern gewaschen.
   Although Gabriel is still a little kid he is definitely sharp as a needle.

2. Wenn du es nicht schaffst das Computer-Programm zu schreiben, ruf einfach meinen Cousin an. Er ist mit allen Wassern gewaschen.
   If you do not succeed in writing the computer program just call my cousin. He is a shrewd customer.

3. Niemand kann Hasenfallen so erfolgreich aufstellen wie George. Er ist mit allen Wassern gewaschen.
   No one can set up traps for rabbits as successfully as George. He knows all the tricks.

---

jemandem nicht über den Weg trauen

---

1. not to trust someone any further than one can see him
2. not to trust someone any further than one can throw him

Beispiel:

1. Manchmal ist es nicht leicht herauszufinden, ob man jemand über den Weg trauen kann.
   Sometimes it is not easy to find out whether someone can be trusted any further than one can see him.

2. Simon ist echt ein Betrüger. Du kannst ihm nicht über den Weg trauen.
Simon is a real swindler. You cannot trust him any further than you can throw him.

---

weiß wie eine Wand sein

---

1. to be as white as a sheet
2. to be as pale as a ghost

Beispiel:

1. Die Camper hatten nicht damit gerechnet, den Bären noch einmal zu sehen, so dass bei seiner Rückkehr alle vor Schrecken weiß wie eine Wand waren.
The campers had not expected to see the bear a second time, so when he returned, all of them were as white as sheets.

2. Offensichtlich ging es dem alten Mann nicht besonders gut. Er konnte nicht mehr sprechen und war weiß wie eine Wand.
Obviously, the old man was not very well. He was not able to speak and he was as pale as a ghost.

---

in ein Wespennest stechen

---

to stir up a hornet's nest

Beispiel:

Selbstverständlich wird die neue Untersuchungskommission in ein Wespennest stechen, wenn auch die älteren Unterlagen als Beweismittel zugelassen werden.
Obviously, if the older documents are admitted as evidence the new inquiry commission will stir up a hornet's nest.

aus allen Wolken fallen

to be thunderstruck

Beispiel:

Als Marina ihrem Mann sagte, dass sie in Zukunft nicht mehr als Lehrerin, sondern als Sozialarbeiterin arbeiten wolle, fiel er aus allen Wolken.
When Marina told her husband that in the future she did not want to work as a teacher anymore but as a social worker, he was thunderstruck.

jedes Wort auf die Goldwaage legen

to take everything to heart

Beispiel:

Er ist so sensibel. Jedes Wort, das man zu ihm sagt, legt er auf die Goldwaage.
He is so sensitive. Every word you say to him he takes to heart.

---

jemandem ein X für ein U vormachen

---

1. to pull the wool over somebody's eyes
2. to make someone believe that black is white

Beispiel:

1. Der Redner war sehr wortgewandt und machte so der gesamten Zuhörerschaft ein X für ein U vor.
   The lecturer was extremely eloquent and thus he pulled the wool over the audience's eyes.

2. Jetzt hat ihre Familie gemerkt, dass Julia ihnen jahrelang ein X für ein U vorgemacht hat. Sie hatte ihnen gesagt, dass sie studiert, während sie tatsächlich als Tänzerin arbeitete.
   Now her family finally realised that Julia made them believe that black is white. She had told them she was studying at university while she was actually working as a dancer.

Z

---
sich die Zähne ausbeißen
---

1. to come to grief
2. to be too hard a nut to crack
3. to bang one's head against a brick wall

Beispiel:

1. An diesem unbestechlichen Lebensmittelkontrolleur wird sich auch unser bester Mann die Zähne ausbeißen.
With this incorruptible food inspector even our best man will come to grief.

2. Herr Jones ist bekannt als sehr anspruchsvoller Professor. An der Abschlussprüfung beißen sich immer fast alle Studenten die Zähne aus.
Mr. Jones is known to be a very demanding professor. The final exam is always too hard a nut to crack for almost any student.

3. Unser Chef mag zwar ein netter Kerl sein, doch mit deiner Bitte um eine Gehaltserhöhung wirst du sicher auf Granit beißen.
Though our boss may be a decent man, you will bang your head against a brick wall by asking for a pay rise.

nicht lange zögern/fackeln

not to let the grass grow under one's feet

Beispiel:

Phil fackelte nicht lange. Er machte Nancy einen Heiratsantrag nachdem sie sich erst eine Woche gekannt hatten.
Phil did not let the grass grow under his feet. He proposed to Nancy after they had only known each other for one week.

jemandem etwas am Zeug flicken

1. to pick holes in something/someone
2. to find fault with someone

Beispiel:

1. Manche Leute sind nie zufrieden mit meiner Arbeit und versuchen ständig mir etwas am Zeug zu flicken.
Some people are never content with my work and constantly try to pick holes in it.

2. Egal wie sehr unser Junge sich bemüht, mein Mann flickt ihm immer etwas am Zeug.
It does not matter how hard our boy tries, my husband always finds fault with him.

sich ins Zeug legen

to get to work with a will

Beispiel:

Wir haben nicht viel Zeit zu verlieren und sollten uns gleich ins Zeug legen.
We do not have much time to loose so we should get to work with a will immediately.

sich die Zunge verbrennen

1. to put one's foot in one's mouth
2. to open one's mouth too wide

Beispiel:

1. Frage ihn nicht danach, wie seine Geschäfte gehen, außer du verbrennst dir gerne die Zunge.
Do not ask him about how his business is going unless you want to put your foot in your mouth.

2. Ich hatte völlig vergessen, dass Ramona ja keine Arbeit hat. Mit meiner Frage nach ihrem Urlaub verbrannte ich mir die Zunge.
I had completely forgotten that Ramona was unemployed. When I asked her about her next vacation I opened my mouth too wide.

das Zünglein an der Waage sein

to tip/turn the balance/scales

Beispiel:

Würden Sie gerne über die Frage diskutieren, ob in einem demokratischen System die Stimme jedes Einzelnen das Zünglein an der Waage sein kann?
Would you like to discuss the question whether, in a democratic system, the vote of each individual may tip the scales?

in der Zwickmühle sein

1. to be in a quandary
2. to be stuck between a rock and a hard place
3. to be in a fix
4. to be in a catch 22 situation

Beispiel:

1. Zugegeben, wir sind in einer Zwickmühle: Greifen wir an, handeln wir rechtswidrig, warten wir, wird die Situation immer gefährlicher.
Admittedly, we are in a quandary. If we attack, we act illegally; if we wait, the situation gets more and more dangerous.

2. Alleine und ohne Geld und Papiere an der Autobahnraststätte war Boris ganz schön in der Zwickmühle.
Sitting alone at a motorway service area without money and his documents, Boris was definitely stuck between a rock and a hard place.

3. Hätte ihm doch jemand gesagt, dass sein neuer Chef mit seiner Ex-Freundin zusammen ist, so wäre er jetzt nicht in der Zwickmühle.
If somebody had told him that his new boss was going out with his ex-girlfriend, he would not be in the fix he is in now.

4. Er war in der Zwickmühle: Er konnte entweder die Katze überfahren oder ihr ausweichen und sein Auto zu Schrott fahren.
He was in a catch 22 situation: he could only run over the cat or dodge it and wreck his car.

fünf Minuten vor Zwölf

at the eleventh hour

>Beispiel:
>
>Es ist fünf vor zwölf – wenn wir die Treibgasproduktion nicht endlich einschränken, vergrößert sich das Ozonloch noch mehr.
>*We are at the eleventh hour – if we do not reduce the production of greenhouse gas the hole in the ozone layer will continue to grow.*

REGISTER

able to take a joke 90
after a fashion 81
all Greek to somebody 13
Alpha and Omega 5
apple pie order 16
as broad as long 48
as thick as thieves 73
at one's wit's end 58
at the 11th hour 119
at the end of the tether 58
bang one's head against a brick wall 114
bark up the wrong tree 45
beat about the bush 15
beat somebody black and blue 38
bet one's sweet life on something 35
birthday suit 6
bite the bullet 7
blow one's own trumpet 59
blurt it out 99
bull in a chinashop 23
burst laughing 57
buy for a song 72
buy for next to nothing 72
call a spade a spade 54
carry coals to Newcastle 24
carry off the prize 105
catch 22 situation 118
catch red-handed 96
catch some z's 69
change hands 12
chip in 75
chip off the old block 45
closed book 16
coast is clear 59

cock and bull story 49
come into the open 26
come rain or shine 34
come to grief 114
count one's chickens before they are hatched 11
cross one's fingers 18
cross one's t's and dot one's i's 5
cut off one's nose to spite one's face 29
cut out for something 34
dance to somebody's tune 73
disappear into thin air 103
do blindfold(ed) 58
do one's bit 75
do one's level best 61
done for 103
draw the line somewhere 54
drop a brick 28
drop in the ocean 98
Dutch treat 53
eat one's hat 11
expecting 101
feast for the eyes 8
feather one's nest 83
feel like a gooseberry 80
find fault 116
fit as a fiddle 28
fit like a glove 6
fit to a T 6
fly in the ointment 39
full of beans 91
get carried away 54
get into hot water 65
get out of bed on the wrong side 31
get some shuteye 69
get the hang of something 37
get the short end of the stick 56
get to work with a will 116
give oneself airs 106

give s.o. a piece of one's mind 60
give someone hell 43
give short shrift 77
give someone the boot 97
give the show away at once 99
give to think about 19
go Dutch 53
grin and bear it 62
hand in glove 44
handle someone with kid gloves 22
haul someone over the coals 27
have a bee in one's bonnet 47
have a bone to pick 46
have a finger in the pie 40
have a lot on one's plate 70
have a say 40
have from the source 78
have had it 103
have hollow legs 24
have one's cake and eat it 44
have one's heart in one's boots 42
have the gift of the gab 64
have the knack 14
have the upper hand 68
heart goes into his boots 42
henpecked husband 72
hold a pistol to somebody's head 61
hungry one could eat a whole horse 62
in a fix 118
in cahoots 19
in hot water 96
in league 19
in more than one place at one time 44
in somebody's shoes 41
in the family way 101
itching to get on with something 65
jump... out of the frying pan 81
keep a stiff upper lip 70

keep in with somebody 107
keep one's fingers crossed 18
keep up appearances 88
keep within bounds 54
kill two birds with one stone 29
kill with kindness 30
king of the hill/mountain/castle 68
know all the tricks 107
know the ropes 86
last straw 99
laugh up one's sleeve 25
lay by for a rainy day 51
lead someone by the nose 32
left out in the cold 56
let bygones be bygones 36
let the dust settle 36
like a foreign language 13
like chalk and cheese 95
line one's own pocket 83
live for the here and now 95
live for the present 95
live it up 83
live on/off the fat of the land 83
look as though butter would not melt in one's mouth 102
make a clean sweep 97
make a mountain... 63
make a song and dance 35
make it hot for someone 43
make one's pile 83
make s.o. believe that black is white 113
meddle in someone else's affairs 40
meet one's match 60
nail one's colours to the mast 26
nip sth. in the bud 53
not able to stand something/somebody 82
not bad at all 23
not to let the grass grow under one's feet 115
not to trust someone any further 108

not worth a straw 75
odd man out 80
on the wrong track 45
once in a blue moon 50
open one's mouth too wide 117
paint someone black 17
pale as a ghost 109
pick holes 116
pillar to post 76
plain sailing 16
play fast and loose 89
play safe 67
play someone's game 73
pleased as Punch 87
pour money down the drain 33
preying on one's mind 65
prick up one's ears 69
pull/make faces 37
pull one's weight 75
pull s.b.'s leg 10
pull the wool over somebody's eyes 113
put a spoke in s.o.'s wheel 55
put all eggs into one basket 52
put in one's two bits 88
put on a brave face 62
put one's foot in it 28
put one's oar in 88
put oneself in a spot 65
put the cart before the horse 74
put things back on the rails again 51
put things straight 51
put through its paces 43
quandary 118
quell sth. at the source 53
reveal one's true colours 26
rule the roost 68
run in the family 25
say yes to everything 48

see eye to eye 44
see how the land lies 41
sell like hot cakes 89
send someone packing 97
sharp as a needle 107
show a clean pair of heels 91
shrewd customer 107
sight for sore eyes 8
six of one and half a dozen of the other 48
sleep like a log 89
smell a rat 14
smooth sailing 16
spitting image 35
splash one's money about 33
square peg in a round hole 76
standing on one's head 58
stark naked 6
stay in someone's good books 107
stick one's oar in 88
stir up a hornet's nest 110
storm in a tea cup 93
straight from the horses mouth 78
stripped to the bone 6
stuck between a rock and a hard place 118
swallow one's pride 85
swallow the pill 7
swear like a fishwife 82
take advantage of someone 9
take everything to heart 112
take liberties with someone 9
take s.o. for a ride 10
take the cake 105
take to one's heels 91
talk s.b.'s ear off 12
talk through one's hat 12
tall stories 49
teach a lesson 19
tell in a roundabout way 13

tell in a veiled language 13
tempest in a teapot 93
thieve like a magpie 79
third wheel 80
thorn in one's side 20
throw a spanner 55
throw into the street 100
throw money away 33
throw out 100
thunderstruck 111
tip/turn the scales/balance 117
too hard a nut to crack 114
top dog 68
treat someone very gingerly 22
turn a blind eye 8
turn out 100
two peas in a pod 21
unable to make head or tail 86
under petticoat rule 72
up to the eyes in work 70
up with the lark 26
upset the apple cart 92
vanish like magic 103
walk like a cat on hot bricks/tiles 22
wear the heart on one's sleeve 41
white as a sheet 109
wind-bag 85
wipe the floor with someone 27
with one arm tied behind one's back 58